Fact Finders®

W9-BWJ-965

PEOPLE YOU
SHOULD KNOW

RUTH BADER GINSBURG

Get to Know the Justice Who Speaks Her Mind

by John Micklos, Jr.

CAPSTONE PRESS
a capstone imprint

Fact Finders Books are published by Capstone Press,
1710 Roe Crest Drive, North Mankato, Minnesota 56003
www.mycapstone.com

Copyright © 2019 by Capstone Press, a Capstone imprint. All rights reserved.
No part of this publication may be reproduced in whole or in part, or stored in a
retrieval system, or transmitted in any form or by any means, electronic, mechanical,
photocopying, recording, or otherwise, without written permission of the publisher.

Library of Congress Cataloging-in-Publication Data
Library of Congress Cataloging-in-Publication data is available on
the Library of Congress website.

ISBN 978-1-5435-5528-8 (library binding)
ISBN 978-1-5435-5926-2 (paperback)
ISBN 978-1-5435-5538-7 (eBook PDF)

Editorial Credits
Mari Bolte, editor; Kayla Rossow, designer; Svetlana Zhurkin, media researcher;
Tori Abraham, production specialist

Photo Credits
Collection of the Supreme Court of the United States, 7, 9, 11, Steve Petteway, 23;
Dreamstime: Lei Xu, 13; Getty Images: Bettmann, 14, MCT/The Collection of the Supreme
Court of the United States, cover, The Washington Post/Nikki Kahn, 26; Newscom:
Reuters/Gary Cameron, 4, Reuters/Larry Downing, 25, Reuters/Lucy Nicholson, 28,
Reuters/Pool/Ken Heinen, 21, Zuma Press/Jim West, 22, Zuma Press/Mark Reinstein, 19;
Shutterstock: Christopher Penler, 27, Rob Crandall, 17
Design Elements by Shutterstock

Source Notes
p. 5, line 8: Shelby County v. Holder. Cornell Law School Legal information Institute. https://www.
law.cornell.edu/supremecourt/text/12-96. Accessed 3 May 2018.

p. 8, line 12: Joe Morgenstern. "'RBG' Review: Courting Progress." https://www.wsj.com/articles/rbg-
review-courting-progress-1525370016. Accessed 9 August 2018.

p. 9, line 17: Ruth Bader Ginsburg. My Own Words. New York: Simon & Schuster,
2016, p. 23

Printed in the United States of America.
PA48

MARTIN COUNTY
LIBRARY SYSTEM

TABLE OF CONTENTS

I DISSENT

Supreme Court justice Ruth Bader Ginsburg could hardly believe it—in June 2013, the Supreme Court decided on a key part of the Voting Rights Act. This act protected the right to vote. Overturning that part would allow states to change their election laws whenever they wanted. They could make it more difficult for **minorities** to vote.

The Supreme Court voted 5–4 against the act. Chief Justice John Roberts announced the majority opinion. He said that the country had changed since the act was first passed in 1965. **Racism** in voting was no longer a major problem, and Congress didn't need to be involved.

Voting rights activists turned out to hear the ruling on *Shelby County v. Holder.*

Ginsburg disagreed. She believed in protecting peoples' right to vote. She filed a **dissenting** opinion, giving recent examples of race-based voter **discrimination**. These, she said, explained why the act remained important. Stopping the act just because the situation had improved was unwise. She compared it to "throwing away your umbrella in a rainstorm because you are not getting wet."

Her dissent was unusually strong. But after more than 50 years as a lawyer and judge, Ginsburg does not fear sharing her opinions. She believes in speaking out for the rights of all people—especially those who have been denied basic rights such as voting.

DID YOU KNOW?

In 1993 Ruth Bader Ginsburg became only the second woman ever appointed to the U.S. Supreme Court. The first, Sandra Day O'Connor, was appointed in 1981.

minority—a group that makes up less than half of a large group

racism—the belief that one race is better than others

dissent—to disagree with the opinion of others

discriminate—to treat people unfairly because of their sex, gender, skin color, class, age, or religion

OVERCOMING DISCRIMINATION

Joan Ruth Bader was born in 1933. She used her middle name in school to stand apart from the other Joans.

Standing out in school was important. Ruth's mother, Celia, had not gone to college. Her family sent Ruth's uncle instead. Celia was determined that Ruth should have that opportunity. Ruth loved learning. She especially loved reading and writing. She was drawn to strong female characters such as Nancy Drew. She also admired Amelia Earhart, the famed female pilot.

Ruth knew sadness growing up. Her older sister, Marilyn, died when Ruth was just a toddler. Her high school years were difficult because her mother was battling cancer. Despite that, Ruth remained active. She took part in student government, twirled a baton, and played cello in the orchestra.

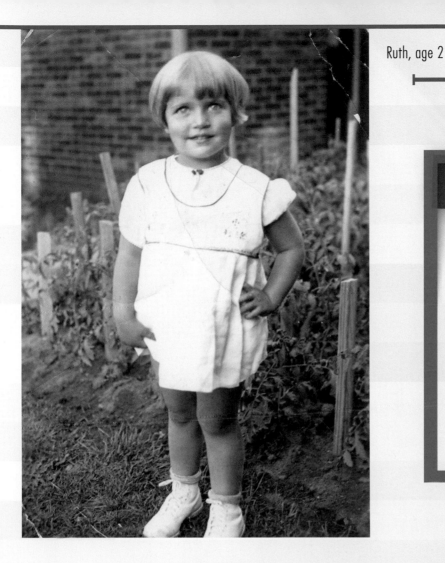

DID YOU KNOW?

In eighth grade, Ruth wrote an essay for her school paper. In it, she described how documents such as England's Magna Carta and the United States' Declaration of Independence shaped the freedoms we have today.

Ruth worked hard and earned several academic awards and a scholarship to Cornell University. She was invited to give a speech at her high school graduation in June 1950. But her mother died just before the event. Ruth stayed home to comfort her father. She left for college that fall determined to fulfill her mother's dreams for her future.

Fulfilling that dream proved challenging. Women in the early 1950s faced discrimination in higher education. There were very few female students. Most male students did not care if their female classmates were smart. They only cared if they were pretty.

Ruth met Martin Ginsburg on a blind date. He was a year ahead of her at Cornell. Martin thought she was cute, but even more importantly, he liked her intelligence. She later said Martin was "the first boy I ever knew who cared that I had a brain." They started out as friends. Over time, they fell in love. They married in June 1954, just after Ruth graduated from college. She was first in her class.

DID YOU KNOW?

Not long after Ruth and Martin were married, Ruth made a tuna casserole for dinner. Martin thought it tasted awful. He took over the cooking and let Ruth focus on other things.

While at Cornell, Ruth took a class in **constitutional** law. She found the course fascinating. Her professor, Robert Cushman, hired her as a research assistant. He taught her that legal skills could help address the problems facing the United States. She decided she wanted to become a lawyer. In November of her senior year, she published her first "legal argument." She argued against using **wiretapping** to gather evidence in a criminal case. She said that the benefits of wiretapping were "outweighed by the general harm it may well do."

Martin and Ruth shortly after their wedding in 1954

constitutional—having to do with an important set of rules or laws, as for a nation

wiretap—to place a device on a telephone line that allows conversations to be heard secretly; used to get information

9

3 ▶ BECOMING A LAWYER

But law school would have to wait. Soon after their wedding, Martin was **drafted** by the U.S. Army. Then in 1955, Ruth had a baby, Jane. After Martin's military discharge in 1956, both Ruth and Martin entered Harvard Law School. Ruth was one of only nine women in a class of 500 students.

Ruth had to juggle difficult law classes and baby Jane. When Martin grew seriously ill, she cared for him as well. Many people would have felt overwhelmed. Not Ruth. She was in class from 8:30 a.m. until 4:00 p.m. Then she had "children's hour" until Jane went to sleep. After that, she focused on studying. She even made time to serve on the *Harvard Law Review*, a student-run publication. Editors were chosen based on their grades. She often worked late into the night. She still does.

draft—to select young people to serve in the military

Ruth's law school career took another turn when Martin graduated in 1958. He was hired by a New York law firm. Ruth decided to finish law school at Columbia University. That allowed her to stay with her husband. Ruth graduated first in her class in 1959. She felt ready to make a difference in the world. But was the world ready for her?

Martin, Jane, and Ruth in 1958

A Few Good Women

Until 1967 women accounted for fewer than 5 percent of the seats in U.S. law schools. In the 1950s many professors resented female law students. Once, Ruth was even asked to justify the law school spot she was "taking away" from a male student. But times have changed. Today nearly 50 percent of law students are women.

A top student and a hard worker, Ruth seemed to have all the qualities an employer would want. But she also had two qualities employers didn't want—she was a woman and a mother. In those days, law firms simply didn't want to hire female lawyers, especially ones with families. Finally, she found a job serving as a law clerk for a U.S. district judge.

In 1963 Ruth started teaching at Rutgers University Law School in New Jersey. While at Rutgers, Ruth taught a course about women and law. She hoped to inspire future female lawyers. Both her career and her family were growing. Her second child, James, was born in 1965.

DID YOU KNOW?

When Ruth was pregnant with Jane, her boss found out. He decided she couldn't attend a training session and **demoted** her to a lower position. Ruth wore loose clothing to hide her pregnancy while at Rutgers. She was afraid she would be fired. James was born in the summer, before the school year began.

Founded in 1766, Rutgers is the eigth-oldest university in the United States.

In 1972 Ruth started teaching at Columbia University Law School in New York City. It is one of the nation's top law schools. She taught there for more than a decade, and became the school's first female **tenured** professor. During that time, she also accepted another challenge that would propel her law career in an exciting new direction.

Equal Pay for Equal Work

When Ruth began teaching at Rutgers University, there were fewer than 20 female law professors in the United States. She earned less than male professors at Rutgers. At first, she didn't complain. But later, she and other female professors sued the university. They won their case.

demote—to give someone a lower rank, usually as a punishment

tenure—a status granted to a teacher after a trial period

4 ADVOCATING FOR WOMEN—AND OTHERS

In the 1970s Ruth helped the American Civil Liberties Union (ACLU). They looked for cases that could advance the cause of women's rights. In one case, they represented Sharron Frontiero of the U.S. Air Force. She had been denied housing and medical benefits for her husband, Joseph. However, servicemen automatically received those benefits for their wives. A lower court ruled against her. Her lawyers **appealed** the decision. The case went before the Supreme Court.

Joseph and Sharron Frontiero, 1971

14

Ruth had never argued such a high profile case before. She was very nervous. But she made the male justices understand that **gender**-based discrimination affects everyone, and won the case.

Still, Ruth was disappointed. The Court had previously ruled that race should not be a reason for restricting people's rights. She wanted the Court to make an equally broad statement about gender. The Court ruled that in this case gender had been improperly used to deny someone's rights. The justices did not, however, extend that same gender protection across all situations.

The Supreme Court

The U.S. Supreme Court is the nation's highest court. Its decisions are final. In most cases, the Supreme Court hears cases that have already been argued before a state supreme court or a lower federal court. The Supreme Court will hear a case if important legal issues are involved.

appeal—to ask another court to review a case already decided by a lower court

gender—the behavioral, cultural, or emotional traits typically associated with one sex

Through the 1970s, Ruth argued six cases before the Supreme Court. She won five of them. Most involved women's rights. But Ruth cared about protecting the rights of all people.

In one case, a man whose wife had died in childbirth took time off work to care for his infant son. At the time, men typically earned most of their family's income. If the men died, their wives received **Social Security** benefits to care for their children. These were known as "mother's benefits." The man requested them for himself. He was denied.

Ruth agreed to take the case. It went before the Supreme Court in 1975. She argued that gender-based discrimination hurt everyone. Again she won. Although this case involved a man, it also helped support the case for women's rights.

Ruth enjoyed the thrill and challenge of arguing cases before the Supreme Court. What would it be like to be a judge?

Social Security—a federal insurance program that provides benefits to retired people and those who are unemployed, disabled, or widowed or widowers

The United States Supreme Court building was finished in 1935. It is where all Supreme Court cases are heard.

By the end of the 1970s Ruth had become a successful lawyer. Becoming a judge was the next step. Lawyers argue cases. Judges preside over cases. This means that they listen to both sides and then make a decision.

Most judges were white men. When President Jimmy Carter took office in 1977 he vowed to change that. He appointed a number of women and African Americans as judges. In 1980 Carter asked Ruth to serve as a judge on the U.S. Court of Appeals in Washington, D.C.

DID YOU KNOW?

Between 1976 and 2002, male and female judges with the U.S. Court of Appeals made similar rulings in over 7,000 cases—except in cases of gender discrimination.

Working as a Team

Martin always supported Ruth. As Ruth's career blossomed, he stepped in and took care of the children. When she was appointed to the Court of Appeals, he moved to Washington, D.C., with her. He was a successful tax lawyer. But he realized that Ruth's career was even more special. He worked behind the scenes to make sure she was considered for the Supreme Court.

President Bill Clinton announced Ruth's nomination to the Supreme Court on June 14, 1993.

In 1993 President Bill Clinton had the opportunity to fill a Supreme Court seat. He considered several people, but he knew within 15 minutes of interviewing Ruth that she was his choice. The Senate's role is to "advise and consent." That means its members question and then vote on whether to confirm all Supreme Court nominees. The Senate confirmed her appointment by a vote of 96 to 3. She became the first Jewish woman and only the second woman in history to serve in this role.

5 ▸ A SUPREME ASSIGNMENT

Supreme Court justices all work to uphold the ideas set forth in the U.S. **Constitution**. Justices who are **conservative** interpret the Constitution as it was first written. They try to stay close to the original meaning and intent. **Liberal** justices view the Constitution as a living document. They tend to adapt their interpretation to today's setting. These differences can lead to heated discussions. Still, the justices try to respect each others' opinions even when they disagree.

Ruth's support of issues such as gender equality and workers' rights mark her as a liberal. She often clashed with conservative justice Antonin Scalia when he served, from 1986 to 2016. Still, she and Scalia became close friends. They shared many interests, including a love of opera. They even had an opera written about their unusual friendship. In it, their characters sing a duet. "We are different, we are one."

Supreme Facts

- The Supreme Court met for the first time in 1790. John Jay served as the first chief justice.
- The number of justices was settled at nine in 1869.
- As of 2018, there have been 17 chief justices and 113 associate justices.
- William O. Douglas was the longest-serving justice, holding his position from 1939 to 1975. The average term is 16 years.
- Justices traditionally wear black robes because black is a solemn color.
- The oldest justice was Oliver Wendell Holmes Jr., who retired at age 90.
- Thurgood Marshall was the first African American justice. He was appointed in 1967.
- Sandra Day O'Connor was the first female justice, appointed in 1981.
- William Howard Taft served as both U.S. president from 1909–1913 and chief justice of the Supreme Court from 1921–1930. He is the only person to have held both positions.

From left: Justices Ruth Bader Ginsburg, David Souter, Antonin Scalia, John Paul Stevens, John Roberts, Sandra Day O'Connor, Anthony Kennedy, Clarence Thomas, and Stephen Breyer in 2005

Constitution—legal document that describes the basic form of the U.S. government and the rights of citizens

conservative—someone who believes in tradition and is cautious about change

liberal—someone who favors progress and reform

21

Ruth continued to support equal rights. In 1996 she heard *United States v. Virginia*. A young woman sued for the right to attend Virginia Military Institute (VMI), the last all-male university in the nation. A district court ruled in VMI's favor.

The Supreme Court ruled differently. By a vote of 7–1, the Court ruled that VMI had to let women attend. Ruth was chosen to write the majority opinion. She made it clear that gender equality was a constitutional right.

Ruth was pleased in 2013 when the Supreme Court struck down a federal law denying benefits to married same-sex couples in states where it was legal. She has presided over gay weddings. Then in 2015, the Court ruled that the Constitution guarantees the right to same-sex marriage throughout the United States.

Thirty-one women enrolled at VMI the first year they were allowed, in 1997. In 2017 there were 63.

Justices Sandra Day O'Connor, Sonia Sotomayor, Ruth Bader Ginsburg, and Elena Kagen in 2010

More Women!

Justice Sandra Day O'Connor served as a friend and mentor to Ruth. When Sandra retired in 2005, Ruth was the only female justice for several years. Sonia Sotomayor was appointed in 2009 and Elena Kagan in 2010. When asked how many female justices are enough, Ruth smiled and said, "Nine." After all, the Court was made up of all men for nearly 200 years. Why not all women at some point?

In her 25 years on the Supreme Court, Ruth has heard roughly 2,000 cases. Her favorite cases involve equal rights for all people. Some have been about affirmative action and women's rights. Others focused on the right of gay people to marry and other important issues.

Sometimes Ruth is on the "winning" side of a case. That means the majority of justices voted as she did. Other times her opinion is part of the minority. The justices reach a conclusion and then issue a formal decision. One of the justices is chosen to write a majority opinion explaining the Court's conclusion. Justices who disagree with the decision may issue a dissenting opinion. In this, they explain their reasons for disagreeing.

I'll Take the Case!

The Supreme Court receives requests to hear about 7,000 cases per year. Of those, they actually hear around 80. They decide another 50 without hearing arguments. There are no witnesses and no jury for these cases. The attorneys for each side submit written briefs and oral arguments.

Lilly Ledbetter (second from left, front row) watched President Barack Obama sign the Lilly Ledbetter Fair Pay Act.

In 2006 the Court heard the *Ledbetter v. Goodyear Tire and Rubber Company* case. After decades of work, Lilly Ledbetter found out that she made far less money than men who did the same job. She sued. Lower courts ruled that she waited too long file her lawsuit. By a 5–4 vote, the Supreme Court agreed. Ruth issued a strong dissent. She challenged Congress to pass a law protecting people like Ledbetter. It took time, but Congress listened. In January 2009 President Barack Obama signed the Lilly Ledbetter Fair Pay Act into law.

Over time, Ruth Bader Ginsburg has become known for writing well-reasoned dissents when she disagrees with the Court's decision. Her words are almost always polite. Still, she makes her meaning quite clear. In December 2000 the Court ruled 5–4 to stop the recount of presidential votes in Florida. That ruling decided the election in favor of Republican George W. Bush over Democrat Al Gore. Ruth disagreed with the Court ruling. She noted that federal courts usually deferred to states' decisions in such matters. The Florida courts had voted to let the recount proceed.

DID YOU KNOW?

Ruth is known for wearing collars called *jabots* with her black justice robes. She has a large collection of them, many of which are white. When presenting a dissenting opinion on a case, though, she wears a black and gold collar. She has a gold and pink collar when she presents the majority opinion.

The employee union case has been called the Supreme Court's most important decision of 2018.

In May 2018 the Court heard three cases involving workers' rights. By a 5–4 margin, they ruled that workers may not band together to challenge violations of federal labor laws. Instead, employees who sign employment agreements to **arbitrate** claims must each do so on their own. They may not do it together. Ruth disagreed strongly. She said many workers would be afraid or unable to act on their own. She called on Congress to pass laws to address this issue, as she did in the *Ledbetter* case.

arbitrate—a process of settling a disagreement between two or more people or groups, by a person they choose

A LASTING LEGACY

Although she is short and slender, Ruth has become a larger-than-life figure. People admire her for speaking out on important issues. She even earned the nickname "Notorious RBG." The name is based on the rapper The Notorious B.I.G., who was also known for being outspoken. Slogans proclaim, "You can't spell TRUTH without RUTH."

Ruth has supported a number of human rights issues during her career, including marriage equality.

RBG also stands as a symbol of toughness. She was diagnosed with cancer twice, once in 1999 and again in 2009. Between the two, she missed less than two weeks of work. Likewise, when Martin, her husband of 56 years, died in 2010, she continued to work. Even in her 80s, RBG continues reading and writing late into the night.

Ruth Bader Ginsburg has left a lasting legacy. For more than 50 years, she has worked tirelessly to guarantee equal rights and opportunities for all people. She overcame many obstacles on her own road to success. She hopes her work as a lawyer and judge will make the road easier for others. She often says that she will stay on the Supreme Court as long as she can go "full steam." She believes she still has work to do.

DID YOU KNOW?

RBG keeps fit with twice-weekly exercise sessions. She does push-ups. She lifts weights. She even throws a weighted ball. Her instructor even wrote a book called *The RBG Workout: How She Stays Strong . . . And You Can Too!*

GLOSSARY

adapt (uh-DAPT)—to change when faced with a new situation

appeal (uh-PEEL)—to ask another court to review a case already decided by a lower court

arbitrate (AHR-buh-trayt)—a process of settling a disagreement between two or more people or groups, by a person they choose

conservative (kon-SUR-vuh-tiv)—someone who believes in tradition and is cautious about change

Constitution (kahn-stuh-TOO-shuhn)—legal document that describes the basic form of the U.S. government and the rights of citizens

constitutional (kahn-stuh-TOO-shuh-nuhl)–having to do with an important set of rules or laws, as for a nation

demote (de-MOTE)—to give someone a lower rank, usually as a punishment

discriminate (dis-KRI-muh-nayt)—to treat people unfairly because of their sex, gender, skin color, class, age, or religion

dissent (di-SENT)—to disagree with the opinion of others

draft (DRAFT)—to select young people to serve in the military

gender (JEHN-dur)—the behavioral, cultural, or emotional traits typically associated with one sex

liberal (LIB-ur-uhl)—someone who favors progress and reform

minority (my-NOR-uh-tee)—a group that makes up less than half of a large group

racism (RAY-si-zim)—the belief that one race is better than others

Social Security (SOH-shul si-KYORR-uh-tee)—a federal insurance program that provides benefits to retired people and those who are unemployed, disabled, or widowed or widowers

tenure (TEN-yuhr)—a status granted to a teacher after a trial period that gives protection from dismissal except for serious cause determined by formal proceedings

wiretap (WIRE-tap)—to place a device on a telephone line that allows conversations to be heard secretly; used to get information

READ MORE

Carmon, Irin, and Shana Knizhnik with Kathleen Krull. *Notorious RBG: The Life and Times of Ruth Bader Ginsburg*. New York: Harper, an imprint of HarperCollins Publishers, 2017.

Levy, Debbie. *I Dissent: Ruth Bader Ginsburg Makes Her Mark*. New York: Simon & Schuster Books for Young Readers, 2016.

Winter, Jonah. *Ruth Bader Ginsburg: The Case of R.B.G. vs. Inequality.* New York: Abrams Books for Young Readers, 2017.

INTERNET SITES

Use FactHound to find Internet sites related to this book.

Visit *www.facthound.com*

Just type in 9781543555288 and go.

Check out projects, games and lots more at **www.capstonekids.com**

CRITICAL THINKING QUESTIONS

1. How have women's rights changed since Ruth's childhood?

2. Think of all the Supreme Court cases Ruth has argued or heard. Of the cases you've read about here, which do you think will have the most long-term effect? Using the text and other sources, explain why.

3. What kind of information supports the idea that Ruth Bader Ginsburg has become a larger-than-life figure?

INDEX